Welsh Sheep

WELSH SHEEP

and their

WOOL

John Williams-Davies

*(Department of Farming and Rural Life,
Welsh Folk Museum, St. Fagans)*

Gomer Press
1981

First Impression—August 1981

ISBN 0 85088 964 2

Printed by J. D. Lewis & Sons Ltd
Gomer Press, Llandysul, Dyfed

Er cof am
Benji Williams

Acknowledgements

I would like to convey my grateful thanks to Mr. A. Price, Tanyfedw, Cray; Mr. B. Thomas, Hengae, Llanllwni; Mr. Davies, Boverton Place Farm, Boverton; Mr. K. B. Davies, Danyreglwys Farm, Garthbrengy; Mr. A. J. W. Miles, Caedypaen Farm, Llandegfedd, and to Mr. Peter Murphy, formerly photographer at the Welsh Folk Museum, St. Fagans, for their help in the preparation of this publication.

Contents

Illustrations

Illustrations: 3—Mrs. H. E. Roberts, Pwllheli; 5, 7, 14—Agricultural Press Limited, *Farmer and Stockbreeder*; 11, 12—National Sheep Association, *British Sheep*; 23—Record Ridgeway, Sheffield, *William Marples & Sons Ltd., Catalogue, 1959.* The remaining illustrations are from the National Museum of Wales, Welsh Folk Museum, St. Fagans.

Line drawings by Phil Watkins and Mike Keane.

Domestication and Early Development

Sheep were amongst the first animals to be domesticated, being brought into the service of man as early as 7,000 B.C. All our modern breeds are thought to have been derived from three of the four types of wild sheep which still exist today. By far the most important in this context was the Urial *(Ovis orientalis)* of south-west Asia. It was almost certainly the first sheep to be domesticated, and is the ancestor of the largest number of domestic breeds. The Moufflon *(Ovis musimon)* a small, goat-like animal found primarily on the Mediterranean islands, although less important than the Urial also played a significant part in the formation of many breeds in western and northern Europe. In contrast, the much larger Argali *(Ovis ammon)* of central Asia played a lesser role, only influencing the breeds of its immediate locality. Only the Bighorn sheep *(Ovis canadensis)* of North America and northern Siberia can safely be excluded from the ancestry of domesticated stock.

The Moufflon *(Ovis musimon)*

Initial domestication is thought to have taken place on the steppes of south-west Asia, probably in the area between Lake Arral and the Caspian Sea. From there domesticated sheep spread southwards into Persia and Mesopotamia, and eventually into Europe and Africa. Sheep were first brought to Europe during the Neolithic period by people who settled in the Danube Basin. Remains of their primitive Urial type animals have been found as far west as Switzerland. At the same time other large scale population movements were taking place in southern Europe. These, principally coastal migrations embraced the territory inhabited by the Moufflon with the result that the animal was domesticated and taken to other areas colonized. Sheep were first brought to the British Isles in this way, and isolated pockets of moufflonoid sheep are still to be found in coastal areas throughout western Europe and Scandinavia. Later, during the first millenium B.C. sheep of a different type were brought to the Mediterranean area. 'Ammon's horn wool sheep', a fine-woolled breed of Urial descent first identified in Mesopotamia around 2,000 B.C., became increasingly common in southern Europe. Roman farmers devoted a great deal of attention to the improvement of this breed, and with the extension of the Roman Empire it spread to most parts of Europe. All our modern European breeds have evolved from the admixture of this basic stock.

Domesticated sheep differ from their wild ancestors in a number of ways. Firstly there is a marked loss of pigment in the wool. Wild sheep are brown in colour whereas most domesticated breeds have a white fleece. Changes also occur in the structure of the animal's coat. Wild sheep have a coat formed of two layers: an outer coat of coarse hairs, and an under-coat of finer fleecy fibres. The proportion of outer coat has become progressively reduced leaving modern sheep with only the soft woollen under-coat. Another characteristic of wild sheep was their propensity to shed their coat annually. This was extremely wasteful in terms of wool because sheep would loose their coats over a wide area. Selective breeding against this tendency was impractical at first, for the simple reason that there was no alternative method of obtaining the wool. It was only with the discovery of iron that it became possible to fashion a tool that would shear efficiently. Consequently it became feasible to breed sheep with a continuously-growing fleece which had to be clipped rather than have to depend upon the haphazard practice of collecting wool during the annual moult.

The History of Sheep in the British Isles

Wild sheep have never existed in Britain, and it is probable that the animal was introduced to these islands in its domesticated form by Neolithic settlers during the third millenium B.C. These people were a part of the great coastal migrations then taking place all around Europe. The sheep they brought with them was the Soay, a small, brown, moufflonoid sheep which exists to this day and represents a remarkable living link between wild and domesticated sheep. It closely resembles its wild ancestor the Moufflon, and is itself the progenitor of many of our modern breeds. This primitive animal exhibits many of the pre-domestication characteristics such as brown colouration, a Kempy outer coat, and a tendency to shed its

Soay Sheep

13

fleece annually. Remnants of the breed were originally confined to the tiny island of Soay, part of the remote island group of St. Kilda a hundred miles off the north-west coast of Scotland. After the St. Kildans left their island in 1930 one hundred and seven Soays were transferred to the main island of Hirta, where there is now a feral population of between 1,000 and 1,500 animals. In recent years there has been a resurgence of interest in the breed which has led to the formation of many new flocks. Whilst most have been in farm parks and similar institutions several feral flocks have also been established. The first such flock in Wales was established on the island of Skokholm off the Dyfed coast in 1934. Further flocks followed on Cardigan Island in 1944, Middleholm in 1945, and St. Margaret's Island near Tenby in 1952. Three of these flocks died out during the early sixties leaving Cardigan Island with the only feral flock of Soays in Wales at the present time. The island, now administered by the West Wales Naturalists' Trust, is forty-four acres in size and supports a population of approximately one hundred sheep. Population numbers are regulated by culling which takes place every three or four years, the last one being in 1976 when some forty animals were removed.

After years of being regarded as an archaic curiosity, interest is now being shown in the commercial potential of the breed. Whilst such possibilities might be limited from the point of view of meat production there appears to be a ready market for the wool. Soay wool is very coarse, with a short staple and natural brownish colour. It has always been in demand from specialist craft weavers, and this market has expanded greatly in recent years.

Sheep of a very different kind were brought to Britain during the Roman occupation. The Romans brought with them the white-face, fine-woollen sheep of Urial descent which they had bred so successfully in southern Europe. This was far superior to the Soay and displaced it from the greater part of the country. Although described as a fine-woolled breed, in modern terms it would be more correct to classify it as a medium-wool. It is currently held by many authorities that evolution within this group ultimately led to the development of the fine-woolled sheep of the Middle Ages as well as our modern long and medium-woolled breeds. The only part of Britain where Soay influence persisted was the far west and north where they became interbred with the Roman sheep. The result of this crossing was the tan-faced group of breeds of which the Cheviot and Welsh Mountain Sheep are the most prominent members.

Another infusion of outside blood took place several centuries later with the arrival of the black-faced breeds. It seems probable that these were associated with the Viking incursions of the eighth and ninth centuries. Evidence for this is provided by the fact that the original distribution of the breed in England corresponds closely to the areas of the strongest Danish influence. Little is known of the origin of the breed, but many experts point to horn shape and blood grouping which suggests that it may be in some way linked to the Argali of central Asia.

The distribution of the three types of sheep remained stable until the early nineteenth century. Breeds descended from the Roman sheep occupied most of lowland England; the black-faced breeds dominated in the north-east and East Anglia, and the Soay related breeds in Scotland, Wales and the western peninsulas. All our modern British breeds have developed from this basic stock.

The Role of Sheep in British Farming

Today we think of the sheep primarily as a provider of meat, but this has not always been the case. The sheep is an animal of many potentialities—a source of meat, milk, wool, skin, and manure—each of which has been pre-eminent of different periods in its history.* During the Roman period sheep were kept principally for their wool, and mutton was practically unknown as a food. Roman farmers were very skilled sheep breeders, and made important advances in the development o fine woolled sheep. Such sheep brought to Britain by the Romans gave these islands an enviable reputation for the

*In his book, *A History of Domesticated Animals*, F. E. Zeuner describes one rather barbaric use made of sheep which fortunately was not emulated elsewhere. He writes "Wood was formerly so scarce at Buenos Aires, and cattle so plentiful that sheep were actually driven into lime kilns in order to answer the purposes of fuel. This fact could hardly have been mentioned as credible however undoubted if a decree of the King of Spain prohibiting this barbarous custom were not still present in the archives of Buenos Aires."

production of high quality wool. Dionysius Periegetes writing in the third century A.D. compared the fineness of British wool to a spider's web, and in Diocletian's Edict on prices, an early fourth century tariff list, some British woollen products were priced above all others. After the Romans departed, sheep farming, like most other sectors of the economy, went into decline, but even during the Dark Ages the export trade in wool continued. A letter from Ch~rlemagne to Offa, King of Mercia, written in 796 A.D., although ostensibly complaining about the quality of cloth recently exported to his court implies clearly that a very high standard was expected in British goods of this nature.

However, by the time of the Norman Conquest the position had changed and sheep were fulfilling a different role as providers of milk. Entries in Domesday Book, completed in 1086, demonstrate clearly that sheep were by then viewed primarily as milk animals. Sheep milking, albeit later in a subsidiary role, continued for centuries and indeed persisted in parts of rural Wales well into the present century. In Glamorgan and Powys, for example, it remained an important seasonal task until the First World War. Richly flavoured sheep's milk cheese was a prized delicacy in rural areas, and there is a record of its being sold in Brecon market as recently as the 1940s.

Throughout the early Middle Ages sheep also played a crucial part in the maintainence of soil fertility. In manorial agriculture the practice of sheep-folding formed an integral, and essential part of the farming system. During the day sheep grazed the common pastures returning each night to be penned on the arable land, where they deposited their manure and trod it into the soil. Each pen or fold was a portable structure which was moved at regular intervals to ensure an even spread of treatment for all the land. Little attention was paid to the needs of the sheep under this system, and no specific crops were raised to feed them. To a certain extent the sheep were sacrificed to the needs of the land. They were viewed almost exclusively as agents for improving the soil by manuring and treading, transferring fertility from the common grazings to the arable land. As a result of this comparative neglect the sheep suffered, and medieval records contain many references to high losses of sheep with corresponding fluctuations in stock numbers.

Wool had regained its former pre-eminence by the twelfth century, a position it retained until the Industrial Revolution. Wool, and later woollen products, became the mainstay of the English economy for the next six centuries. Initially most of the clip had been exported to the manufacturing centres of Flanders and Italy, but from the thirteenth century onwards steps were taken to stop this trade and stimulate the domestic industry. Discriminatory taxes were placed on the exports of raw wool, and Flemish weavers were encouraged to settle in Britain and pass on their expertise to the native craftsman. The industry flourished especially in East Anglia and the west of England where a great deal of wealth was generated, a wealth that is still reflected today in the rich architectural heritage of those areas. A much smaller Flemish colony was established in south Pembrokeshire, helping to make that area the premier woollen manufacturing district in Wales for several centuries.

Wool remained pre-eminent until the eighteenth century, when the population growth associated with the Industrial Revolution led to a massive increase in the demand for meat. Steps were consequently taken to realize the meat-producing potential of the sheep, and selective breeding was directed to this end. This was a complete reversal of previous policy because for centuries wool had been the sole consideration of the flock master and the quality of the carcase had been completely ignored. Any sheep, however poor and mis-shapen, was kept as long as it could be shorn, as Lord Ernle put it, 'To the golden fleece the carcase was sacrificed'.* The situation was changed during the eighteenth century by the efforts of agricultural improvers such as Robert Bakewell of Dishley Grange in Leicestershire. By careful breeding, Bakewell transformed the old, slow-maturing, heavy-fleeced Leicester longwool into a compact, quick-fattening animal of great potential. More important perhaps was the new Leicester's ability to transfer this capacity for early maturity to the breeds with which it was crossed. Bakewell's work was given widespread publicity by agricultural writers such as Arthur Young, with the result that attempts were made at crossing Leicesters with practically every breed then in existence. Few of these efforts met with any real success, but

*Ernle, Lord., *English Farming, Past and Present*, London 1922.

there is scarcely a breed existing today which does not contain some measure of Leicester blood. Bakewell's example was enthusiastically followed by others such as John Ellman of Glynde in Sussex whose Southdown rams also came to be used extensively on other breeds.

If demand for mutton gave the farmer the incentive to improve his sheep, the new husbandry of the Agrarian Revolution gave him the means. Enclosure made the improvement of stock almost inevitable and the more intensive farming, incorporating the use of new crops such as turnips and clover, increased the weight of carcase and fleece almost automatically.

Such improvement, however, had a detrimental effect upon the quality of wool. Although farmers were loath to admit it, selective breeding and intensive agriculture proved to be incompatible with the production of fine wool. The Leicester in particular was a rather coarse-woolled breed, and its extensive use had a detrimental effect upon the fleece of many of the breeds with which it was crossed. Criticism of the breed was even more fierce when it was realized that the quality of its mutton was also inferior to that of the old breeds. However, it must be said in Bakewell's defence that his object was not to produce high quality meat for the tables of the rich, but substantial nourishment for the masses. The meat of the Leicester might not have been as well flavoured as that of other breeds, but it was cheaper and found a ready market amongst the working classes.

Nowhere was the deterioration in the quality of wool more apparent than in the case of the Ryeland sheep of Herefordshire. For centuries the Ryeland, which inhabited the heathlands around Ross-on-Wye, had been the best of the fine-woolled breeds, the provider of 'Leominster ore' which had been one of the mainstays of the better-quality products of the English woollen industry. From 1750 onwards attempts were made to increase the weight and fleece of the breed. This was eventually achieved, but only at the cost of the quality of the wool. No less a person than George III, 'Farmer George', took a personal interest in the breed and formed a group to promote its fortunes. Flocks were removed from the rich, heavy lowlands to the lighter heathland soils, which were more conducive to the production of fine wool. Attempts were also made to counteract the coarsening effect of the Leicester blood by crossing with the relatively finer-woolled Southdown. All was to no avail, for by the beginning of the nineteenth century 'the ancient breed was improved into insignificance'. It still exists today, a useful meat-producing animal, but bearing no resemblance to its original form.

Naturally, such a deterioration in the wool was viewed with dismay from many quarters; centuries of reverence for fine wool was not easily dissipated. Such feelings were summed up by William Marshall writing at the end of the eighteenth century, when he commented,

'As an object of national attention, the coat of the sheep is of first importance—and every wilful attempt to supplant it was an act of treason'.

Indeed, in England preoccupation with fine wool became a form of obsessive patriotism, and in 1790 a group of noblemen and gentlemen farmers founded a *Society for the Improvement of British Wool*. Attempts were made to introduce the Merino, the finest-woolled of all sheep into the country; George III himself established several flocks in England between 1791 and 1801. They attained a widespread distribution, but the experiment ultimately failed because the quality of the wool proved to be inferior to that from Spain. Since the small carcase size of the breed made it impractical as a dual-purpose animal the Merino disappeared from the English farming scene during the 1840s.

The revolution in the character of British Wool consisted largely of the coarsening and lengthening of the fibres, making it more suitable for the manufacture of worsteds rather than woollen goods. Wool had merely changed, not deteriorated as contemporary opinion maintained. What had initially appeared as a disaster ultimately worked to the advantage of the British farmer because the nature of the demand also changed. During the second quarter of the nineteenth century the fine-wool sector of the market came to be dominated by colonial and European producers with whom the home producers could not hope to compete. The increase in demand for worsted cloth on the other hand could only be satisfied by the British farmer. The new type of wool might not have commanded the same high price as fine wool, but there was a ready and growing market for it.

By the end of the nineteenth century it could be argued that the pendulum had swung too far, and that the carcase was being given too much attention at the expense of the fleece. This was certainly the view of the woollen manufacturers and the journals of the period abound with complaints that farmers were neglecting their wool and not realizing its full potential. Since the Second World War, however, more attention has been paid to the fleece, and it has been realized that wool, although still of secondary importance, represents an important extra source of income. Most shepherds now pay an equal amount of attention to the weight and value of their wool as they do to their crop of quick-fleshing lambs.

A Survey of Welsh Sheep Breeds

As no standard classification of sheep breeds exists, the Welsh breeds included in this survey have been classified according to their position within the system of sheep farming currently practised in the United Kingdom. This system, directed primarily towards fat lamb production, divides British breeds into four categories:

A.   Mountain Breeds

Hill and mountain breeds are the foundation of the entire system. These hardy breeds are capable of utilizing the hostile mountain environment, turning what would otherwise be a barren wasteland into a reservoir of store animals. Wales, being predominently an upland country, has a large number of representatives in this category. These breeds include the Welsh Mountain (encompassing Hardy Welsh, Improved Welsh, South Wales Mountain, Black Welsh Mountain, and *Defaid Torddu* or Badger-faced sheep), the Beulah Speckled-face, the Brecknock Hill Cheviot and the Hill Radnor.

B.   Crossing Breeds

After a few years in the mountain environment the ewes are drafted to lower land where they are crossed with rams of larger, prolific breeds such as the Blue faced, and Border Leicesters. The Halfbreds thus formed combine the hardiness, healthy constitution, and mothering qualities of their mountain dams with the prolificacy and high growth rates of their sires. Wales has no native crossing rams, but the Border Leicester cross is widely used in the Principality. At one time Wales was also without a crossing ewe, but since the Second World War the Welsh Halfbred, based on a Welsh Mountain—Border Leicester cross has emerged as a distinct breed, and is now one of the most sought after ewes of its type. A second crossing ewe, the Welsh Mule has emerged in the mid-seventies. Based on a Bluefaced Leicester ram—hill ewe cross it is a breed of immense potential. Recent years have also seen the development of a Clun Forest ewe—Border Leicester cross known officially as the English Halfbred.

C. Down Breeds

Down breeds were developed on the rich lands of southern and eastern England primarily for the production of meat. When crossed with Halfbred ewes their offspring is ideal for fat lamb production, being large, quick to mature and providing meat of a very high quality. There are no Down breeds native to Wales although they are now used extensively by Welsh farmers. The most popular is the ubiquitous black-faced Suffolk, although others such as the Ryeland, Dorset Down, Hampshire and Shropshire are also used.

D. Grassland Breeds

One group of breeds remains outside this overall stratification. Grassland or Intermediate sheep form a link between the mountain and lowland breeds. To a certain extent they combine the characteristics of both groups, possessing the hardiness necessary to survive on all but the highest hills and the size needed to utilize richer lowland grazings, but lacking the excellence of the specialist breeds. Formerly such flocks were kept pure, but Down rams have been increasingly used in recent years to improve lamb sizes. Two of the most important British grassland breeds, the Kerry Hill and the Clun Forest, evolved within a few miles of each other on the hills of the Welsh border. Two lesser known but similar breeds, the Llŷn and the Llanwenog, also developed on the western side of the country.

The following section contains a brief description of each breed together with an outline of its history and development, its present role and future prospects. All the breeds included in the survey are native to Wales with the exception of the Brecknock Hill Cheviot which was brought from Scotland in the early nineteenth century. Since that time it has evolved in such a way that it can now be regarded as a distinct breed separate from its parent stock. At first sight the Clun Forest might also appear to be a non-native breed, having been named after the small market town of Clun in Shropshire. The area in which the breed developed, however, embraces extensive areas of north eastern Powys and it is therefore included in this booklet.

A.   MOUNTAIN BREEDS

Welsh Mountain Sheep

Tan-faced sheep resulting from the inter-breeding of imported Roman white-faced sheep and the native Soay have inhabited the mountains of Wales for nearly two thousand years. To this day they remain numerically and economically the most important breed in the country. Little is known of their early development, and detailed descriptions of the breed do not appear until the late eighteenth century. Most of these early accounts were very disparaging; indeed no other breed can have been subjected to such universal condemnation. Agricultural writers of the period, obsessed as they were with improvement, could scarcely find a kind word to say for it. Thomas Rowlandson, for example, noted that 'the sheep in North and South Wales . . . are in every way inferior to the black-faced heath sheep . . . in the flavour of mutton, size of carcase and value of fleece', and Arthur Young quite simply noted that the Welsh sheep was 'the most despicable of all types'. The situation was confused by the fact that at this time Welsh mountain sheep were not a homogeneous breed but encompassed a number of distinctive local strains, some of them very primitive. The most primitive occupied the higher mountains and was described by David Low as being dark in colour, horned in both sexes and with a pronounced similarity to the wild goat in behaviour, reflecting quite clearly its Soay origins. This type disappeared during the nineteenth century, but other local varieties persisted well into the present century. For example, a distinct breed—small, with a white face and brown legs survived on the Presely Hills in Dyfed up to the First World War. It was eventually absorbed into the main body of mountain sheep, but as late as the 1930s examples of the type, known locally as *siwanod*, were common in the district. Another example was *Defaid Rhiw*, an archaic breed found on Mynydd y Rhiw in Llŷn, which was comparable with the mass of mountain sheep prior to improvement. During the 1920s its position was usurped by the Welsh Mountain breed and now it survives only in greatly diminished numbers. Other local varieties such as the Cardi, the Talybont and Llanllwni have all become extinct within the last hundred years.

Rhiw ewe

All the early agricultural writers suggested immediate replacement of Welsh Mountain Sheep as being the only possible method of improvement. Several abortive attempts were made at the introduction of exotic breeds before it was finally realized that this was impractical, because whatever its failings the Welsh was the only breed that was fully adapted to the hostile Welsh mountain environment. Once this crucial fact was appreciated the direction of improvement changed, effort was concentrated upon selection within the breed as the only realistic means of progress. Even then there were numerous obstacles to improvement. Much of the land was too poor to support a larger breed of sheep, increases in size were only really possible if there was a commensurate improvement in the quality of keep. Even selective breeding was hampered by the custom of grazing flocks on common lands. The efforts of individual farmers to improve the quality of their stock were negated by the indiscriminate mating which took place amongst the sheep on the open moorland. Some form of regulation governing the quality of rams allowed on to the common land was urgently required if improvements were to be made. Legislation was slow in coming but in many districts farmers themselves, realizing the advantages to be gained, agreed on voluntary controls to achieve this end. Another, and possibly more difficult barrier to be overcome, was the mentality of the mass of the farming population, with its in-built prejudice to any form of change. Nineteenth century reports abound with complaints about the reluctance of many farmers to countenance improvement, and it appeared to many of the writers that the peasant mentality actually equated poor animals with being the only true ones. An illustration of this attitude appears in an account of the judging of one of the classes at an early show run by the Devynock Agricultural Society. It states that

> 'There was strong objection to the adjudication of the Welsh Mountain ram class . . . It was claimed that there was only one genuine mountaineer in the class. The judge admitted that he had noticed this diminutive ill-shapen animal with its shaggy coat more reminiscent of hair than of wool, but if the local farmers thought this was the ideal to be obtained in the breeding of mountain sheep they had better think again.'

Eventually all the barriers were overcome and by the end of the century marked improvements had been made in the quality of the stock. A Welsh Mountain Sheep Society was established in 1905 with the specific aim of fostering the breed, and under its auspices the first flock book was published in 1906, and the first annual sale of accredited stock held in 1922.

As a result of continued improvement and evolution, three distinct types of Welsh Mountain Sheep are now recognised. The smallest is the HARDY WELSH MOUNTAIN SHEEP which is largely confined to north Wales, where its extreme hardiness and thrift enables it to flourish in conditions too harsh even for other mountain breeds. Mid-Wales is the home of the PEDIGREE ABERYSTWYTH, or IMP-ROVED WELSH MOUNTAIN SHEEP, a larger animal, which although lacking the hardiness of its northern counter-part makes up for it in size and docility which has led to its gaining in popularity during recent years. Glamorgan and Gwent are the home of the SOUTH WALES MOUN-TAIN SHEEP formerly known as the NELSON SHEEP which is the largest of all the types with a tan face, and a coarse

Welsh Mountain Sheep (Aberystwyth or Improved Type)

25

fleece containing red Kempy fibres* which frequently gives the breed it characteristic brown collar.

Despite improvement Welsh Mountain sheep remain the smallest economically significant breed in the United Kingdom, with the weight of adult ewes rarely exceeding forty kilograms. Environmental conditions in the mountains dictate that only the smallest, thriftiest breeds survive, and in such circumstances the Welsh sheep have no serious rivals. Survival demands that the breed not only has to be extremely hardy, but also very active, wandering the open moorland in search of food. On enclosed farms the breed's instinctive propensity to wander is a serious drawback and is largely responsible for its limited popularity on the lowlands. As a mountain breed its commercial importance is as a store animal capable of surviving in the hostile mountain areas. As a function of its role some 450,000 draft ewes are sold from the mountains of Wales each year. The breed requires a minimal amount of shepherding which together with its low purchase price makes it an attractive proposition as a breeding ewe. Since it can also transmit its qualities of hardiness, thrift and mothering to its progeny many ewes are used in the formation of the Welsh Halfbred, which is now recognized as a breed in its own right.

Throughout history the wool of Welsh Mountain sheep has been regarded as inferior, indeed agricultural writers usually described it as 'despicable'. Adverse environmental conditions were primarily responsible for this, the cold, wet climate of the mountains being the antithesis of that required for the growth of fine wool. Such was the harshness of the habitat that the protective function of the fleece had to be given absolute priority with the quality of the wool being very much a secondary consideration. The low temperatures and heavy rainfall promoted the growth of coarse, Kempy wool, and the precarious nature of the food supply led to frequent breaks in the growth of wool, and extreme variations in its quality. Generally the wool had a fairly open staple suitable for working with the primitive machinery available in the nineteenth century. On a commercial level the Welsh woollen industry had concentrated upon the production of a fairly narrow range of goods, of which flannel, a thoroughly-milled

---

*Kemp is a thick inelastic hairy fibre interspersed with wool fibres in a fleece. Most often it is a chalky white although red Kemp is not infrequent: they do not absorb dyes and are usually undesirable.

cloth of simple weave was the most important. It was manufactured widely throughout the country and a large proportion of the total output was exported. Demand for Welsh cloth was largely governed by the dictates of fashion because of the peculiarly coarse nature of the raw material. When rough fabrics such as friezes were in vogue, demand for Welsh cloth was high; when fashion favoured softer fabrics, demand slumped. In an effort to counter the effects of such violent fluctuations in demand, Welsh manufacturers began to buy wool from outside the Principality thereby allowing them to extend their product range. The direct link between Welsh wool and Welsh woollen products was broken, and it has never been re-established.

Over the last hundred years the quantity and quality of Welsh Mountain wool has been improved, and it can no longer be regarded as an unimportant by-product of sheep farming. There has been a threefold increase in the weight of the fleece to an average of three pounds per animal. Quality too has similarly been improved, and although Kemp is still present in the wool it is on nothing like the same scale as was once the case. Many farmers maintain that some Kemp is essential to retain the hardiness of the animal, and it is consequently unlikely that it will ever be completely eradicated. As there is great variation in the quality of wool even within the same fleece there is a corresponding variety of uses made of it, ranging from carpets and rugs to the finest tweeds. Differences also exist between the different types of mountain sheep. The Hardy Welsh produces some three pounds of variable wool, whilst the Improved Welsh produces almost twice as much wool of consistently higher quality. A proportion of this wool combines the softness and strength required in the making of textured knitting yarns, and there is a ready market for some in the manufacture of quality tweeds. The South Wales Mountain on the other hand produces a much coarser fleece frequently containing a high proportion of Kemp and is primarily used in the manufacture of carpets and rugs.

Two economically less significant, but nonetheless interesting members of this breed are the Black Welsh Mountain Sheep and the *Torddu* or Badger-faced sheep.

Black Welsh Mountain ewe

Black Welsh Mountain Sheep

Black lambs occur naturally in flocks of Welsh Mountain
Sheep, and are probably throwbacks to the breed's original
Soay ancestors. Over a hundred years ago some farmers began
selecting such individuals from their flocks as the basis for a
separate breed. The breed was given official recognition in the
1920s, and a Flock Book published in 1922. Black Sheep were
formerly kept exclusively for decorative purposes, but serious
consideration is now being given to the commercial potential
of the breed. With this in mind they have entered and won
many important competitions including the prestigious
Championship of Hill Breeds at the 1973 Royal Smithfield
Show. There has also been a dramatic increase in the numbers
of the breed over the past few years, growing from thirteen
registered flocks containing 300 breeding ewes in 1971, to 135
flocks containing over 1000 breeding ewes in 1975. At the
same time the breed has been greatly refined, and many
experts now claim that they should no longer be regarded as
true mountain sheep. Hardiness has been reduced to such an
extent that it is arguable whether the breed could now survive

in its original habitat. Indeed one correspondent to *The Ark*, the Journal of the Rare Breeds Survival Trust, went as far as to suggest that to call them mountain sheep is now a misnomer, and that the breed could now be more correctly referred to as Black Welsh Park Sheep. Black sheep, of course, still occur naturally in mountain flocks, but these bear very little relation to the pedigree Black Welsh Mountain Sheep as they exist today.

Black wool has always been in demand for speciality purposes. In the Middle Ages it was known as *gwlân coch-ddu* (literally red-black wool) and was much sought after by weavers. The fleece normally weighs some four pounds and has a high quality count approaching 50's.* It is a soft wool, but very hard-wearing and was used extensively in traditional Welsh woollen products such as blankets and shawls, as well as knitting wools and hosiery yarn. The wool requires no dyeing and can be used naturally in checked materials, or mixed with white to form grey yarn. At the woollen mill in the Welsh Folk Museum, for example, wool from the museum's own small flock of Black Sheep is mixed with two parts of white wool to form a grey yarn of remarkably even consistency which is used in the weaving of traditional patterns.

Defaid Torddu or Badger-faced Sheep

Another colour variation which occurs naturally, though less frequently in Welsh Mountain flocks is the *torddu* or badger-faced pattern. Experts agree that it too is a simple recessive patterning arising as a result of the breed's Soay ancestry, the facial marking especially closely resembling those of the Soay. Several other breeds with a similar ancestry such as the Cheviot, Shetland and Norwegian sheep also exhibit the same tendency. The markings are very distinctive, the animal is white with two black stripes running down the face, thereby giving the animal its English name. A broad black band also occurs on the sheep's chest and continues along the underside of the body, giving rise to the Welsh name—torddu, literally 'black belly'. A much rarer occurrence is the *Torwyn* (white-belly) where the colours are reversed. There is some evidence

---

*The fineness of wool is classified according to a system known as the Bradford Count. The higher the value on the scale, the finer the wool. A full explanation of the system is given on page 68.

Dafad Torddu or Badger-faced Sheep

to suggest that *Defaid Torddu* might have been kept as a separate breed at one time, but were eventually absorbed into the main breed. As is the case with other freak occurrences, the presence of badger-faced sheep in a flock was at one time regarded as being a sign of bad luck. Despite this, no specific measures were taken to guard against their occurrence in a flock, although *torddu* rams were never used in breeding. In recent years the *torddu* has gained in popularity, especially for decorative purposes, and attempts have been made to establish them as a breed in the same way as was done with the Black Welsh Mountain Sheep. A Breed Society was formed in 1977, and a class for the breed included in the Royal Welsh Agricultural Society's Show for the first time in 1978.

Beulah Speckled-face

The Beulah, or Epynt Hill Breed as it was formerly known, is larger than the Welsh Mountain breed, and is recognizable as its familiar name suggest by its characteristic speckled face. Whilst the origins of the breed are unclear, it is known that sheep of this type roamed Mynydd Epynt and the hills around the village of Beulah in west Powys well over a hundred years ago. One view is that the breed is the result of a Welsh Mountain ewe—Kerry Hill ram cross, but most experts now believe it to be based on a Mountain ewe—Derbyshire Griststone ram cross. There is clear evidence that Gritstones were brought to the area in the early nineteenth century and there is a remarkable resemblance between the facial characteristics of the two breeds. Official recognition was given to the breed in the early twentieth century, and the Epynt Hill and Beulah Speckle-Face Sheep Society established in 1958. Since that time the breed has gone from strength to strength, and many flocks are now to be found throughout the country.

The breed's present role lies primarily in the production of draft ewes, which produce high quality lambs when crossed

Beulah Speckled-faced Ram

31

with Down rams. Speckle-face ewes are noted as good mothers with a plentiful supply of milk providing for high lamb growth rates. The average lambing percentage for the breed is 175% whilst 200% lambing is not uncommon for flocks of older ewes. As a result of its normal management, whereby the ewe spends a part of the year on enclosed land the breed is far more docile than true mountain sheep, making it a more attractive proposition for the lowland farmer. More recently, strains have been developed within the breed which compare favourably even with Welsh Mountain sheep in terms of hardiness. Welsh Hill Speckled Faces or Hardy Speckled Faces as they are known are both hardier and smaller than the true Beulah, and can live in all but the harshest environments. They have the advantage of being larger than Welsh Mountain Sheep and have steadily been displacing them for many areas, especially in mid-Wales.

Beulah fleeces are clean and soft, averaging three to four pounds in weight with a quality count ranging from 44's to 58's. The finest wool is in demand for the manufacture of high quality fabrics such as soft-handling flannels and tweeds. Coarser woolled sheep can provide up to five pounds of wool, much of which is used in the carpet industry.

Brecknock Hill Cheviot

Cheviot sheep originated on the hills of the Scottish Border Country. Originally it was a small tan-faced breed closely resembling the old Welsh Mountain Sheep to which it was in fact related. During the second half of the eighteenth century New Leicester rams were used very successfully on the breed, with the result that it became one of the best mountain sheep of the period. From its home area the breed spread northwards into Scotland where it vied with the Scottish Blackface for supremacy. Ultimately it became the dominant breed in Caithness, and the Southern Uplands while the Blackface proved to be superior in the harsher Highlands. Caithness Cheviots evolved differently from the parent breed, and now North Country Cheviots, as they are known, are regarded as a breed in their own right.

Wales was seen by many as a country ideally suited to Cheviots, and several attempts were made to introduce them during the early years of the nineteenth century. The first such

Brecknock Hill Cheviots

attempts were made in Glamorgan by improving landlords
such as Rees Williams of Aberpergwm, and in 1820 the Misses
Bassett of Llanelay were commended by the county Agricultural Society for their experiments with the breed. It was in
south-west Powys, however, that the breed became most
firmly established, and where it remains the dominant breed to
this day. Scottish settlers were attracted to the area during the
enclosure of the Great Forest of Brecknock in the 1820, and
they brought with them Cheviot rams which were used on the
native ewes. By 1865 the breed was sufficiently well-estab-
lished in the locality to justify its inclusion as a separate class in
the first Defynnog Agricultural Show held in that year. Many
attempts have since been made to introduce the breed into the
surrounding areas. All have been unsuccessful, for the
Cheviot, which thrives on the Old Red Sandstone soils on the
northern slopes of the Brecon Beacons barely survives when
moved to the poorer Coal Measures just a few miles to the
south. The history of no other breed demonstrates so clearly
the peculiarly close and complex relationship which exists
between the sheep and its environment.

The Brecknock Cheviot has changed to such an extent over

the years that it can now be regarded as a breed distinct from its original Cheviot ancestors. A breed society was formed in 1970, and the breed which had also been known locally as the Sennybridge Cheviot given the official title of Brecknock Hill Cheviot. It is a medium sized sheep producing good mutton, and excellent lamb when crossed with Down rams. Although developed primarily as a meat producing animal it also gives five to six pounds of good quality wool. The fleece is white, dense, uniform in quality (with a spinning count between 48's and 56's) and remarkably Kemp-free for a mountain breed. Most Cheviot wool is used in conjunction with that of other breeds in the production of Scottish tweeds, but it is impossible to determine what proportion of Brecknock Hill Cheviot wool is used for this purpose.

Hill Radnor

The Radnor's origins are obscure and complex. One view is that it is descended from a strain of the original Welsh Mountain sheep, but others assert that it is based on an older Radnor breed improved by crossing with Shropshires and Cluns, with the addition of Kerry Hill blood at a later date. It is a small, active sheep with a brownish face and a characteristic light grey patch around the nose which is taken by many breeders to denote hardiness in the animal.

As its name, Hill Radnor, implies, it is primarily a mountain sheep although some claim that it could be better classified as an intermediate breed. It is not as hardy as the Welsh, but the kinder climatic conditions of its native hills do not make such hardiness necessary. On the other hand it has many advantages over the Welsh. The quality of its wool is very high for a mountain breed, and its docility makes it much easier to keep in an enclosed area. In its native south-east Powys it was often kept in conjunction with flocks of Welsh Mountain sheep, and the farmers who practised such a system, when questioned as to their preference invariably rated the Radnor higher than its rival. Despite this, the Radnor has been loosing ground steadily in recent years because of one great drawback—the very slow growth rate of its lambs. Under the traditional farming system geared to the production of four-year-old wethers for mutton the breed prospered, but now that the demand is for quick-fattening lambs it can no longer

Hill Radnor Sheep

compete. As a result, the breed is in decline, even in its native territory.

Traditionally the sheep of the Radnor Forest have been famed for the quality of their wool. Walter Davies* quotes a local saying:-

> 'O bont y Clas i blwy'r Bugeildy
> Y mae'r gwlân rhywioca yng Nghymru'

[From Glasbury Bridge to Bugeildy Parish is to be found the finest wool in Wales]
Whilst it might no longer be the finest wool in Wales, it is still remarkably good quality for a mountain fleece. In fact, the Radnor probably has the lowest proportion of Kemp of practically any mountain breed. Of course some Kemp is present but this does not detract from the wool, but gives the fleece a slightly rough feel which makes it suitable for the manufacture of textured fabrics. A large proportion of Radnor wool is consequently used in the making of high class tweeds, flannels, and other items requiring a slightly rough finish.

*Davies, W., *Agricultural Survey of South Wales, Volume II*, London, 1815.

B.   CROSSING BREEDS

Welsh Halfbred

The term halfbred denotes a first cross of pure breeds. It was first applied in the specific sheep rearing context to the progeny of a Border Leicester-Cheviot mating. Now its use has been extended to Wales, where the name Welsh Halfbred is applied to the progeny of a Welsh Mountain ewe and Border Leicester ram. The emergence of the Welsh Halfbred as a recognized breed, and the rapid and continued growth in its popularity ranks as one of the most significant developments in Welsh agriculture over the past twenty years. Welsh Halfbreds are bred each year from Mountain ewes that have proven mothering qualities, having successfully reared several crops of lambs under rigorous mountain conditions. Such ewes are drafted to the lowlands where they are crossed with Border Leicester rams. Only the best ewes are used for breeding, and standards are maintained by the Welsh Halfbred Sheep Breeders Association which runs the official breed sales, and ensures that the stringent rules governing the breed are adhered to.

Welsh Halfbred ewe

Welsh Halfbred ewes are compact, medium-sized sheep with the characteristic aquiline head of the Leicester breed. The ewes exemplify the commercial value of hybrid vigour in their performance and productivity, combining the thriftiness, hardiness and mothering qualities of their mountain dams with the size and docility of their Border Leicester sires. They are extremely economic and easy to manage requiring the minimum of hand-feeding, and are ideal for high levels of stocking. At the present time the ewes are normally crossed with Down rams for the production of early fat lambs, many of which are ready for marketing within nine weeks. The breed also exhibits a propensity for twinning, normally giving a lambing percentage in excess of 150%. It was this combination of high fecundity and early maturity which led to the breed taking three out of the four National Performance Awards given by the Meat and Livestock Commission in 1978. Another of the breed's advantages is that it can successfully rear a catch crop of lambs in its first year, and frequently goes on to produce eight or nine crops of lambs during its lifetime. Demand for Welsh Halfbreds has been such over recent years that there have not been enough breeding ewes available to satisfy it.

Despite the fact that the breed was developed primarily for meat production it also provides good quality wool. Fleeces vary in weight between five and eight pounds with a medium staple of five to six inches, and a quality count ranging from 38's to 54's. It is mostly used to supply the hosiery industry, although a proportion also goes into the manufacture of knitting yarn.

The Welsh Mule

The Mule or Greyface is the progeny of a Bluefaced Leicester ram and a hill ewe. Bluefaced rams were in fact specifically developed for the purpose of crossing with hill ewes; indeed the ideal Bluefaced Leicester ram can be described quite simply as one which produces first class Mule lambs. It is the most prolific breed, and is not uncommon for pure bred flocks to return a lambing percentage in excess of 300%. In addition it can transmit this prolificacy together with its other qualities of early maturity, fleshing, and longevity to its offspring. When these qualities are combined with the hardiness, vitality and

The Mule

milking qualities of hill ewes it provides breeding ewes of great commercial importance. In fact, it is probably true to say that the Mule is the most outstanding commercial sheep readily available to sheep farmers in Great Britain.

The Mule was first developed in northern England using predominantly Swaledale ewes although other breeds such as the Scottish Blackface are also used. During the past decade the northern Mule has spread to Wales where it has become established, often at the expense of the Welsh Halfbred. This prompted many farmers to experiment with the production of a Welsh Mule using Welsh Mountain, Beulah, Brecknock Hill Cheviot, and Hardy Speckled face ewes. All these proved moderately successful, but the Hardy Speckled face cross appears to have the greatest potential. A Welsh Mule Society was formed in 1979 with an original membership of sixty breeders, a number that has since increased to 270. The first official breed sale, held in September of that year at Welshpool attracted a catalogue entry of 4,000 ewes. Two sales were held in the following year with a combined entry of almost 10,000 ewes, and it is hoped to double this number in the current year.

Performance tests are now being carried out on the Welsh Mule and although initial impressions are favourable it is as yet too early for any reliable figures to be produced. However, if the performance of the northern Mule can be taken as a guide the new breed should have the advantage over the Welsh Halfbred in several respects. Firstly, the Mule reflects the Bluefaced Leicester's prolificacy and has an average lambing between 175% and 200% with figures well over 200% not being uncommon. When crossed with Down rams the Mule also produces slightly larger, leaner lambs more suitable for today's market, especially the export trade. In many cases the lambs can also be sold, directly off the mother because of the ewes remarkable milking ability. Initial comparisons show that the Mule produces slightly less wool than the Halfbred although no information is yet available for wool quality and the uses to which it is put.

C. DOWN BREEDS

None of these are native to Wales.

D. GRASSLAND BREEDS

Kerry Hill

The Welsh border region presents an extremely complicated picture in terms of the history and development of its sheep breeds. As Trow Smith states in his *History of British Livestock Husbandry*—

'The complex of sheep breeds in this area—Staffordshire, Shropshire, Radnor and Montgomery—was a tangle of horns and polls; black faces, white faces, and intermediate types: as complicated as the geological structure of the region, and perhaps, partly allied to it and to the rapidly changing environments'.

To illustrate this, he lists the polled grey-faced sheep of Cannock Chase, the Longmynd, the Morse Common and numerous others. Out of this tangle of breeds and types there eventually emerged two breeds which were to have a profound impact on the sheep farming world—the Kerry Hill and the Clun.

As long ago as 1809. Walter Davies noted the presence of a distinctive breed of sheep on the hills around the village of Kerry in north-west Powys. The role this played in the formation of the modern day Kerry Hill, however, is the subject of some controversy. Recent evidence suggest that it was in fact no more important in this context than a number of other breeds which existed in the locality. Clun Forest to the east, for example, was inhabited by a 'dirty speckled-face' sheep; Longmynd and Long Mountain to the north both had breeds famed for their fine wool, and Epynt to the south a sheep with distinctive facial marking almost identical to those of the modern Kerry. It was from this melting pot, with the addition of Shropshire Down blood at a later date, that the present breed eventually emerged. Even as late as 1850-60 there was little uniformity in the breed, and many people regarded it as just a larger than average Welsh Mountain sheep. During the last quarter of the nineteenth century, however, determined efforts were made to stabilize and improve the breed, culminating in the formation of a Breed Society in 1892 and the publication of the first flock book in 1899.

The breed is both striking and attractive in appearance. It has a bold upright carriage, and very distinctive markings in the form of clearly defined black patches around the nose, and eyes, and also around the knees. Breed specifications state that a black muzzle is obligatory, but that the markings on the eyes and knees are optional and largely a matter of fashion. The current vogue is for very pronounced marking, contrasting sharply with the photographs of Kerrys taken earlier this century which frequently show animals with almost white faces. Many breeders now fear that the fashion has been taken too far, and that such overemphasis on black markings could lead to dark fibres appearing in the fleece, a very serious fault. Necessity could well dictate that future breeding will have to be directed towards reducing the size and intensity of the markings.

One of the breed's most important virtues is its adaptability to different farming situations. It is equally at home feeding on lowland leys as it is on the poor grazing of its native hills, whilst on wetter lands it is said to have no peer. Naturally the type of animal varies with the environment: Kerrys kept on the

Kerry Hill Sheep

uplands are scarcely larger than Welsh Mountain sheep, whilst those which have spent their lives in richer surroundings frequently approach Down breeds in size. The breed also has a high prolificacy, ranging from 175% to 200% lambing, which allied to its mothering abilities makes it a popular breed for fat lamb production, especially when crossed with Down rams. Despite these qualities the breed's popularity has waned somewhat in recent years as it has come increasingly into competition with other breeds, notably the Clun. The Clun's improved mothering qualities and quicker fattening lambs in fact makes it a serious threat to the Kerry's future. Even at markets such as Knighton in the very heart of its territory, where the breed had formerly constituted 90% of all sheep sales, reports now state that the proportion of Kerrys sold has dropped to less than half the total turnover. Devotees of the breed claim that this is merely a cyclical decline in the breed's fortune, many farmers changing for change's sake. Others argue that economic forces make the changeover far more than a temporary phenomenon, and that the breed is set for a marked and steady decline in its fortunes.

Walter Davies described the Kerry Hill as being '. . . the

only breed in Wales that produces perfect wool', and whilst its present wool may not be perfect, it is nevertheless of very good quality. The fleece, weighing an average of five pounds, is very white, dense, of good length and remarkably Kemp-free. It has a spinning count of 54's to 56's, and is classed with the Down breeds in the higher categories of British wool from the marketing point of view. Extensive use is made of Kerry wool in the manufacture of the finest quality tweeds and blankets, whilst its whiteness makes it eminently suitable for dyeing the very delicate pastel shades much used in the manufacture of hosiery and knitting yarns. A proportion of the wool also goes into the production of heavier materials such as industrial felts.

Clun Forest

The other important breed to emerge from the Welsh border-west Midlands complex is the Clun Forest, whose ancestry is similarly unclear. Most experts now agree, however, that it is an amalgam of the 'ancient white-faced Clun', itself a product of the Ryeland-Radnor complex, to which a large infusion of Shropshire blood was added at a later date. It was very slow fixing as a breed, and despite the fact that a class for Clun sheep was included in the Shropshire Agricultural Society's Show as early as 1875, it was still being reported twenty years later that there was 'a want of unanimity' amongst breeders, as to face colour and other important characteristics. Even the 1909 edition of George Stephens' *Book of the Farm* states that the Clun should be regarded as a type rather than a breed. Stabilization eventually came with the formation of a Breed Society in 1925, but it was not until after the Second World War that its potential was fully realized. Between 1945 and 1965 the number of registered flocks grew from 100 to 1,100, and by 1976 it was estimated that there were more than 40,000 breeding ewes in the United Kingdom alone. It is the proud boast of the Breed Society that there is not a county in England and Wales without a flock of Cluns, and in addition large numbers have been sent to many overseas countries.

It has often been said that the Clun was bred in the nineteenth century to twentieth century specifications, and in the context of modern farming systems it is an extremely important breed. Although it was developed as an intermediate breed its remarkable post-war popularity has been due to its potential in the lowland setting. This was only possible because of the adaptability of the breed, it being equally at home on roots, ley grassland, even under hand-feeding in intensive farming systems as it is on its native hill grazings. The Clun has a lambing percentage averaging 173% (with 60 to 80% of the yearling ewes bearing lambs), which combined with its excellent mothering capability makes it a much sought-after breeding ewe. Recognition of this led to the Clun becoming the dominant stock used in the development of two of Britain's most recent high-performance breeds, the Colbred and the Cambridge. Pure bred Clun lambs meet modern requirements but where the true excellence of the breed shows is in the production of quick-fattening lambs by one of the Down sires. Another advantage the breed has over many of its rivals is the ease with which it can be managed. Its docility, low mortality rate, and freedom from lambing problems make it one of the least demanding breeds to shepherd. Finally, there is the breed's profitability which could well prove to be the crucial factor in the long term. In these days of cost-conscious agriculture any breed that is not profitable could soon find itself relegated to fanciers and farm parks. The Clun with its relatively low purchase price, cheapness of keep, and high

Clun ewe with lambs

return on capital outlay is in no such danger. This above all is what has led to its current popularity, and why it has begun to displace many other less efficient breeds.

Clun Forest sheep are reputed by many to have the finest wool in Britain. The fleece, averaging five to seven pounds in weight is very dense, white, and free from Kemp and black fibres. It is one of the easiest fleeces to sort, for with the exception of a small proportion of coarse britch the quality of the wool is uniformly high with a spinning count of 58's. Whilst this is not as high as that of Commonwealth breeds, Clun wool has a superior 'life' and springiness which gives it an advantage in the manufacture of high quality specialist fibres. Most goes into the making of fine hosiery and knitting yarns although some of it is used in the production of industrial felts. A ready market for Clun wool exists not only in the United Kingdom but also many European countries, including some behind the Iron Curtain.

Llŷn

Early attempts at improving Welsh sheep by crossing with rams of the new English breeds met with little success. One of the rare exceptions was the Llŷn breed which originated on the Llŷn Peninsula and also became established on the island of Anglesey. Walter Davies testified to the existence of a larger-than-average type of sheep on Anglesey in 1810, but gives no information as to their origins. Tradition and the records of prominent local breeders suggest that the breed was based on Roscommon rams, imported from Ireland during the mid-eighteenth century. Most authorities now, however, tend to attribute the foundation of the breed to Richard Lloyd Edwards of Nanhoron, a local squire and improving landlord, who crossed native Welsh ewes with Border Leicester rams some half a century later. The modern appearance of the Llŷn certainly testifies to the use of Leicester stock at some stage in its development, and many put the proportion of Leicester blood in the breed as high as 70%.

The breed produces lambs of satisfactory carcase size with a good quality fleece. Its greatest attribute, however, is its prolificacy with a lambing percentage averaging some 150%. Individual members of the breed have achieved quite outstanding lambing performances, one ewe producing eighteen

Llŷn ewes with their lambs

lambs in five crops. Despite this the breed has been somewhat neglected, and until recently remained relatively unknown outside its native Gwynedd. Within its home area its role, like that of the other grassland breeds, is now primarily for crossing with Down rams to produce fat lambs. In this role it compares favourably with the most popular of grassland breeds, the Clun. However, because of its smaller size and remote location, it has never achieved the widespread popularity of its borderland counterpart which was ideally placed to extend its territory into the English lowlands. Its potential has now been realized, however, and many new flocks have been established in areas well away from its original home. Llŷn ewes, like Clun ewes, were also used as part of the foundation stock for the development of the Cambridge breed, evidence that its potential is now appreciated in many quarters.

Llanwenog

The Llanwenog is a compact sheep with a plain black wool-free face, but with a prominent tuft on the forehead. It was formed during the late nineteenth century by crossing Shropshire Down rams with a primitive, horned, black-faced sheep

Llanwenog ewe

which formerly inhabited the hills around the village of Llanllwni in Dyfed. Although this latter breed has been extinct for
over half a century isolated throwbacks are still being reported
in long established flocks in the locality.

Like the other intermediate breeds, the Llanwenog is suited
to a variety of habitats ranging from the rich lowlands of its
native Teifi Valley to the more meagre grazings of the
surrounding hills. In many respects the breed resembles the
Clun, but like the Llŷn sheep to the north, the Llanwenog has
never received the same recognition as its borderland counter-
part, the Clun. The reasons for its comparative neglect are also
similar, namely its smaller size, and the remoteness of its
original home from the lowland plains. The greatest attribute
of the breed is its prolificacy, and it has during recent years
achieved consistently high placings in lambing competitions,
including winning the Wool Marketing Board Trophy for the
highest lambing percentage in 1965 with the remarkable
average of 230 lambs per 100 sheep. This high prolificacy led
to the Llanwenog too being used in the formation of the Cambridge breed. Pure bred Llanwenog lambs are adequate for
present day market tastes, but it too is increasingly being

crossed with Down rams in an attempt to obtain larger lambs. Increasing interest is now being shown in the breed and flocks of Llanwenog sheep are to be found well outside the Teifi Valley, including one at the Welsh Folk Museum at St. Fagans.

A Llanwenog fleece contains on average between four and five pounds of medium-stapled wool of very high quality. It has a uniformly high spinning count, between 56's and 58's, and a very soft handle which makes it eminently suitable for the manufacture of high quality materials such as knitting yarns and fine tweeds. At the Welsh Folk Museum it is used in the making of traditional blankets and shawls.

Harvesting the Wool

Washing the sheep

Formerly it was the custom to wash sheep before they were shorn, a practice which was advantageous to the farmer in two ways. He received an enhanced price for washed wool, and on a more practical level the removal of accumulated dirt from the fleece made shearing easier. After washing, which took place in early summer, the sheep were given a few days to dry thoroughly before being sheared. It was a belief in many districts that sheep had to be shorn within nine days of being washed otherwise they would become soiled and the operation would have to be repeated.

Gathering the sheep for washing was usually the most laborious part of the whole operation especially in mountainous districts where the flocks were scattered over a wide area of open moorland, and a measure of co-operation between farms was often necessary to accomplish the task. On the Sugar Loaf Mountain near Abergavenny in south-east Powys, for example, the first Wednesday in July was the traditional gathering day. Farmers assembled at a pre-determined spot and then began clearing the mountain, each farmer driving his sheep in the direction of his own farm. On the other hand, on the slopes of Carnedd Llywelyn in Gwynedd where a similar system was practiced, all the sheep from a particular area of the mountain were driven into a communal fold where they were sorted by their respective owners before being taken to the farms.

Washing facilities varied enormously from place to place ranging from the purpose-built covered washeries, such as the one at Llysworney in the Vale of Glamorgan, to the temporarily dammed local brooks which served the same purpose on the majority of farms. Most farmers made do by damming a small stream with earth or stones to form a pool adequate for their needs. The size of the pool was unimportant, provided it contained a depth of more than three feet of water which was considered the absolute minimum required for successful washing. A drop of a few feet into the water was also essential to ensure that the sheep became fully submerged as they plunged into the pool. A gently sloping grassy bank of the opposite side was also desirable as it allowed the heavy, water-logged sheep to climb easily from the water without becoming soiled. More permanent stone or concrete washeries were built by some farmers and these often came to be used by all the neighbouring farmers. Areas with a high proportion of common grazing often had a communal washery such as the one near Crymych in Dyfed. This was used by the commoners who were all obliged to prepare and maintain it in return for its use.

Far more unconventional means of washing were employed by some farmers—there are numerous examples of bridges being used for this purpose. Sheep would be driven on to the bridge, one end of which had been blocked to form a pen from which they were thrown over the parapet into the river. Where the drop was too great the animals were lowered into the river using a makeshift rope harness. This practice came to an end as a result of the increase in road traffic: travellers were reluctant to wait before they could cross the bridge, and farmers were equally reluctant to remove the flock until the job had been completed. Although sheep were normally washed in small streams, larger rivers were used in some places such as in the River Teifi at Cenarth in Dyfed. Here the strength of the current was such that coracles were employed to ensure that the sheep reached the opposite bank in safety. This picturesque custom, which had become something of a tourist attraction, continued until recently. At one time it was also common for sheep to be washed in the sea. Lisle described the practice in

Washing sheep in the River Teifi at Cenarth, Dyfed, 1933

eighteenth-century Kent, and there is evidence of its continued existence in the Llŷn Peninsula up to this century. There the sheep were carried a short distance out to sea and made to swim back to the shore. The one serious drawback with this method was that sheep washed in salt water took much longer to dry.

Unlike the present time when farmers are content just to let their sheep swim through the washery once or twice, the older farmers insisted on a far more thorough cleansing. In the period before the First World War it was often the custom to have men actually in the water washing each sheep individually. These men were amply compensated with a liberal supply of beer or whisky which ensured that there was no lack of volunteers for this wet and unpleasant task. In some places men stood in large barrels which had been placed in the water, an ingenious system which allowed them to wash the sheep as before, but hopefully without getting soaked in the process. Widespread use was also made of an implement known as a paddle, a long handled tool with a short T-piece at one end, which could be manipulated by a person standing on the bank

Washing sheep at Llanbedr, Powys

Washing sheep using paddles, Glanusk, Powys, *c* 1930

to plunge the sheep under the water and to ensure that they found the right way out.

Despite the importance formerly attached to the task, washing was not an unmixed blessing from the farmer's point of view. Newly washed sheep were particularly susceptible to illness should there be a sudden deterioration in the weather, and there are many instances of heavy losses being incurred. Neither were the financial benefits as clear cut as at first appears, for whilst it was true that washed wool attracted a higher price, this was offset by the fact that the total weight of wool to be sold was reduced by the removal of impurities during washing. On arable land for example where sheep were particularly prone to soiling, up to 20% of the total weight of wool could be lost in this way. When the substantial labour costs involved in the operation are added to this it becomes clear that a large price differential was needed between washed and unwashed wool to make the practice financially viable. As financial considerations grew more important during the twentieth century an increasing number of farmers abandoned the practice. A few gave up as early as the 1920s, but the majority continued into the fifties and sixties before following suit. Some farmers made a rational decision to give up washing based on price comparisons between washed and unwashed wool, but the majority appear to have simply followed the example of opinion leaders in their areas. In many areas the discontinuation of washing coincided with the changeover to mechanical shearing, for it was much easier to cut unwashed wool with a machine than it had been with hand shears. During recent years an increased premium has been paid for washed wool, which has enticed some farmers to resume washing, but at this stage it is too soon to predict whether the practice will become as widespread as formerly.

Shearing

Shearing time was the busiest period in the sheep farmers calendar involving a great deal of hard work both in preparation and in the actual shearing itself. The shearing area had to be cleared and cleaned, storage space prepared, temporary pens erected and the equipment inspected. After washing, most farmers tried to keep their sheep convenient to the farm but where this was impossible the flock had to be gathered from the mountain once more. If this could not be done the previous evening gathering had to take place in the very early hours of shearing day morning to ensure that the work could begin at a reasonable time. With the increasing availability of farm buildings in recent years there has been a growing tendency to keep the sheep in the night before shearing. This not only saves valuable time in the morning but has the added advantage of keeping the flock dry in the event of overnight rain.

When shearing was done by hand the traditional method of doing the work in most districts was for the shearer to sit astride a low wooden bench with the sheep placed on its back in his lap. He began by clipping the wool from the animal's underside. Once this was complete the sheep's feet were bound, then starting at the neck and following the line of the ribs the left flank was shorn as far as the backbone. Finally, the animal was turned and the other flank clipped, this time cutting from the backbone towards the belly. Care was taken throughout to ensure that the fleece remained in one piece.

There were, however, many local departures from this pattern. In south-east Wales, for example, it was customary for the shearer to stand behind his bench with the sheep in front of him, whilst in some areas benches were not used at all and the animal placed on the ground. Some farmers in Pembroke-shire tied a loop of string around the shearing bench and this was placed over the hind legs of the sheep to prevent it struggling whilst its underparts were being shorn. The whole subject of tying the animal's feet during shearing was in fact a matter of debate. Many lowland farmers did not do so, main-taining that it was in some way an admission of lack of skill on the part of the shearer. Upland farmers countered this argument with the claim that mountain sheep, although smaller, were far wilder than their lowland counterparts and needed tying as much for their own safety as for ease of shearing. Normally all four feet were bound, but in some places one leg was left free because it was believed that this was more comfortable and less dangerous for the sheep. It also appears that at one time there were differences in the actual method of shearing. Walter Davies writing in 1815 states that in Dyfed sheep were shorn longitudinally along the body rather than following the line of the ribs. This appears to have been a less expeditious technique, however, for Davies states that only thirty to forty sheep could have been shorn in one day using this method, whereas over fifty could be done in the same time using the normal method.

Shearing was a craft which required a high degree of skill,

Shearing scene near Dolgellau, Gwynedd, *c* 1910

Shearing at Llangurig, Powys

and one in which its practitioners took justifiable pride. Each sheep had to be evenly shorn, with parallel swaths running around the body, whilst cutting the skin and causing the animal to bleed was considered a cardinal sin. Many took pride in the speed with which they worked, the fastest shearers being capable of shearing a sheep in a little over two minutes, although five to ten minutes was the time taken under normal circumstances. Factors other than the proficiency of the shearer had to be taken into account because some sheep were far easier to shear than others. The condition of the animal was one important factor, a well fed sheep in the peak of health being much easier to shear than a poor one.

Shearing made heavy demands upon labour, requiring approximately one man to every forty sheep. In addition, other workers were needed for a variety of ancillary tasks. For example, a large sheep farm in Cwm Prysor, near Traws-fynydd, Gwynedd, needed the following to support the twenty or so shearers:

2 to supervise the sheep pens

3 to catch the sheep and carry them to the shearers

2 to provide ties to bind the feet

2 to roll up the fleeces

2 to pack the wool

1 to mark the sheep

1 to release the sheep after shearing.

On lowland farms where sheep numbers were low and labour relatively plentiful, shearing could comfortably be completed by the farm's own staff. In upland areas on the other hand the situation was very different. Sheep numbers were high and the nature of the farming such that the normal labour requirements was low thus making the provision of extra staff for a seasonal peak of demand such as shearing very difficult. To overcome this problem farmers joined together in co-oper-ating groups shearing at each farm in turn. The degree of formality involved in such arrangements varied from district to district. In the Mynachlog-ddu district of Dyfed for example, the farmers were only loosely bound together: there was no given order of shearing, the date at each farm being determined by discussion amongst the participants on a day to day basis, and even reciprocity, a fundamental feature of co-operative groups was not as rigidly adhered to as elsewhere. At the other end of the spectrum the system could be seen at its most rigid in the Tregaron-Abergwesyn areas on the borders of Dyfed and Powys. Here rules evolved over generations were strictly observed. Each farm had an ascribed shearing day which remained unchanged from year to year. Such was the inflexibility of the system that should a farm miss its turn for whatever reason it had to go to the end of the queue. Some farms in this area had so many sheep that even co-operation could not satisfy their demand for labour, and they had to resort to hiring extra help from neighbouring towns and villages. Scores of youths from Tregaron, Abergwesyn and Rhandir-mwyn spent the entire shearing season of some three weeks in the mountain, moving from farm to farm, being hired on a daily basis. Nantstalwyn, the largest farm in this area with nearly four thousand sheep, needed more than a hundred shearers to carry out the work. A total of well over two hundred people assembled at Nantstalwyn for shearing, which even then needed two days to complete.

Not all mountain farms made such heavy demands on labour, but most had large numbers of people assembled on shearing day, making it an important social occasion especially in the isolated districts where the widely scattered population and long distances between farms inhibited social contact. Shearing, unlike other co-operative tasks, had the advantage of being an activity where participants worked in close proximity to one another, making it an ideal opportunity for telling stories and exchanging information. In many areas a barrel of beer or cider was an essential accompaniment to the labour, although for the safety of both sheep and shearer this was often withheld until late in the day. Often the men stayed on after the work was completed and spent the evening chatting or singing, whilst the younger people played games such as quoits or participated in weight-lifting competitions. There were so many people present at Nantstalwyn, near Tregaron, that it was usual for an impromptu concert or eisteddfod to be held on the farm.

Shearing day was an equally important occasion for the women of the household, and the lavishness of the food provided for the company was a matter of great status in the

Shearing day company, Troedrhiwcymer near Llanddewibrefi, Dyfed, 1912

local community. Housewives vied with each other in the preparation of food, and the men looked forward to the shearing feasts as one of the culinary highlights of the year. Many farmers slaughtered a wether or even a steer for the occasion, and traditional shearing day dishes such as *cacen gneifio* (shearing cake), a yeast cake similar to Christmas cake, and *pwdin cneifio* (shearing pudding), a rich rice pudding with added fruit, were served in many areas. The midday meal was usually taken in the farmhouse kitchen, often in shifts when the number of people present was too large. This was a time of great teasing and banter between the men and the women who waited upon them. Throughout the day there were frequent breaks for refreshments, and often a large supper would be provided if the work continued into the evening. Such was the social importance of the occasion in many areas that technological advances in shearing methods were resisted because of the threat they posed to the custom.

Technological changes in shearing methods

Hand shears had been the only efficient shearing tool since their invention in the Iron Age. Originally they resembled large scissors in shape, but during the late eighteenth century these were gradually replaced by spring-tined shears which consisted of two steel blades connected by a ring-shaped spring. Prior to the mid-nineteenth century shears had been made by village blacksmiths in a variety of styles which suited the local conditions, with the result that a large number of distinctive regional types had evolved. But, during the nineteenth century large manufacturing companies such as Isaac Nash of Stourbridge, and Wards of Sheffield came to dominate the market replacing the locally made product. However, such was the attachment of many farmers to their traditional patterns that the large firms were obliged to reproduce these designs in their own products. In the late nineteenth century, therefore, anachronistic names such as Prysor pattern shears, or Merioneth pattern shears appear in catalogues of tools mass-produced in Sheffield. Rationalisation was a slow process and it was not until well into the twentieth century that local patterns were replaced by two or three standard designs.

The first steps in mechanizing the work were taken in Australia, where the large numbers of sheep and a desperate

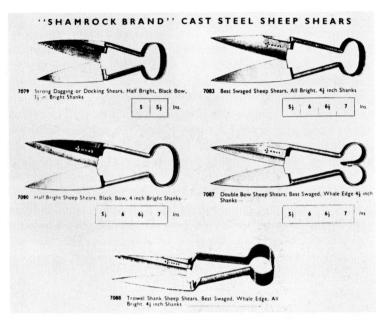

7079 Strong Dagging or Docking Shears, Half Bright, Black Bow, 3½ in Bright Shanks

| 5 | 5½ | Ins. |

7083 Best Swaged Sheep Shears, All Bright, 4½ inch Shanks

| 5½ | 6 | 6½ | 7 | Ins. |

7080 Half Bright Sheep Shears, Black Bow, 4 inch Bright Shanks

| 5½ | 6 | 6½ | 7 | Ins. |

7087 Double Bow Sheep Shears, Best Swaged, Whale Edge 4½ inch Shanks

| 5½ | 6 | 6½ | 7 | Ins. |

7088 Trowel Shank Sheep Shears, Best Swaged, Whale Edge, All Bright, 4½ inch Shanks

Hand shears from the catalogue of William Marples Ltd., Sheffield, 1959

shortage of skilled labour made shearing a massive problem. As early as 1868 a certain James Higham perfected a mechanical clipper, which remains the prototype for shears to this day. Unfortunately, at that time no suitable motive power was available and its potential remained unfulfilled for the best part of twenty years. By the 1890s, however, the necessary advances in drive systems had been made to make hand-turned shearing machines a practical proposition. In 1893 the Royal Agricultural Society of England put on a trial of such devices at its Chester meeting of that year. In subsequent years the Society's journals contain regular references to shearing machines and the many improvements being made in their design.

But, farmers remained sceptical and slow in adapting the machine. This was understandable to an extent, because at that stage in its development the hand operated machine did not really represent a significant improvement in terms of efficiency. It was only marginally faster than handshearing and needed two men to operate. Only when a shortage of skilled men began to be felt during the First World War did

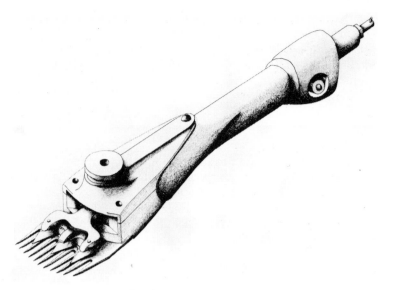

Mechanical shearing head

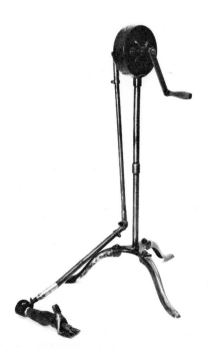

A *Cooper Stewart* hand operated shearing machine

such machines come to be used in any numbers. Unskilled labourers could be employed to turn the machine whilst all the skilled men concentrated on the actual shearing. Like all new ideas the shearing machine had to face its share of hostility and prejudice. Many of the older farmers felt that the machine cut far too close to the skin leaving the sheep unprotected in the event of a sudden change in the weather. Widespread losses were forecast and this served to delay its acceptance especially in some mountain districts.

Advances were constantly being sought in motive power, and experiments with compressed air driven machines were being conducted as early as the 1890s. The real breakthrough came with the advent of the smaller oil and petrol engines, such as the Lister and the Villiers from the 1920s onwards, which provided a reliable and cheap source of mechanical power. A later adaptation was a machine which could be driven off a tractor, and the process culminated with the use of the electric motor, which is almost the universal source of power today. Some areas, such as Gwynedd where there

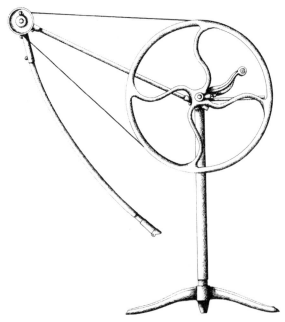

Hand operated, belt driven shearing machine manufactured by *Burman & Sons Ltd.*, Birmingham

was no shortage of skilled shearers and where shearing was an important social occasion, continued to use the hand shears well into the 1960s. The early hand driven machines were viewed with derision in these areas, and it was not until the advent of the more efficient sources of power, allied to the decline in the availability of skilled shearers that the change-over occurred.

The technique initially employed in shearing with a machine was simply an adaptation of the traditional hand shearing method. Again innovation came from the southern hemisphere, this time from New Zealand where considerable effort had been devoted to the development of the most efficient method of shearing. The technique they evolved differed considerably from the traditional method. The shearer

Modern day shearing, Cynllwyd, Gwynedd

used fewer, longitudinal strokes along the sheep's body rather than the short strokes following the line of the ribs as had been the custom. Such is the economy of the method that a proficient shearer can complete a sheep in under a minute, less than half the time previously taken. The New Zealand style, as it became known, was introduced to Britain in 1957 when the British Wool Marketing Board invited Godfrey Bowen, the chief instructor for the New Zealand Wool Board, to the United Kingdom to promote its use. Since that time it has been the principal method taught at agricultural colleges and by Young Farmers Clubs and has now replaced the old technique, especially amongst the younger farmers.

Most Welsh farmers have now abandoned the practice of shearing their own flocks, preferring to pay specialists to do the work. During the shearing seasons gangs of highly skilled shearers, many of them from the southern hemisphere countries, travel the Welsh countryside moving from farm to farm. They are contracted to shear at so much per head, and such is the speed with which they work that they can earn relatively large sums of money in a short time.

Packing the wool

After the fleece has been cut, it is rolled in preparation for packing. In most areas this is done by placing it flat on the floor (which has been cleaned or covered for that purpose) with the outside uppermost. Both sides are then folded inwards and starting at the tail end, it is rolled into a cylindrical shape some eighteen inches in width, and a little less in depth. The remaining neck wool is twisted into a rope which is wound around the fleece and tied into a loose knot. A low table was used for rolling in some areas which did away with the back breaking work of kneeling over the fleece on the floor. A different method was employed in southern Gwynedd where the fleece was rolled by a person standing up holding the fleece in front of him with the tail-end tucked under his chin. He folded in the sides of the fleece and rolled it up a foot or so at a time until the process was completed as before. Some wool merchants maintained that the practice of twisting the neck wool into a rope was detrimental to the wool especially if it was turned too tightly. To counter this some farmers bound their fleeces by wrapping the neck wool around the fleece without

Rolling up a fleece

twisting it first. A trick tried by some farmers to improve the appearance of their wool was to roll the fleece the other way with the neck wool innermost thus disguising the presence of red Kempt which was most prevelent in this area.

The fleeces were packed immediately on some farms, but the normal practice was to store them until there was more time to carry out the work. Most farmers merely threw the fleeces haphazardly into a storage bay although some took great care in stacking it with the best fleeces visible on the outside. Again the effectiveness of this ploy in deceiving the experienced wool buyer is somewhat doubtful. Wool was packed into large purpose-made sacks for selling which could hold up to two hundred weight. In recent years these have been provided by

Traditional method of tying a fleece

the wool merchants, but at one time the farmer had to provide
his own, which he did often by sewing together a number of
smaller sacks.

Selling the Wool

Farmers had traditionally disposed of their wool through the
local woollen mills, often on a non-commercial basis, the
factory owner retaining a proportion of the wool as payment
for the work. As rural areas became less isolated this practice
declined, although the mills continued to play a part in the
process, often acting as local agents for larger manufacturers
elsewhere. Wool fairs were an alternative method of sale in

some parts of Wales. One such fair was held at Pembroke in the second week of June each year. Local farmers brought their wool to the market hall where it was sold to buyers, mostly from the Teifi Valley, an important manufacturing centre some thirty miles to the north. Sales here were by private treaty, but elsewhere were often by auction. For example, in the old county of Denbighshire 80% of all wool sales during the 1920s were by auction. Many farmers favoured this and believed that a higher price could be obtained by such a directly competitive method.

The most common method of selling wool over the greater part of the country, however, was through the specialist wool dealers a number of whom operated in each district. Most farmers remained loyal to the same buyer each year, and the dealer provided them with sacks which they filled and delivered to a specified place for weighing. Although these sales were by private bargaining, there was very little room for negotiation and prices closely reflected current market levels. The only option open to a farmer who was not satisfied with the price offered was to keep his wool in the hope of obtaining a higher price at a later date. Many farmers did this and it was not unknown for farms to have two or three years wool in storage waiting to be sold. Upon reflection, however, most farmers agree that this was not a wise practice: a lot of storage space was occupied, the quality of the wool deteriorated, and in the majority of cases recorded the wool had ultimately to be sold at a price lower than that originally offered.

During this period several attempts were made by farmers to by-pass the middle man in order to obtain a better price for their wool. Some farmers, especially those who had easy access to the railway began to deal directly with the manufacturers. They took their wool to the station, recorded its weight, saw that it was dispatched properly and received their payment in due course. One group of farmers in the Newtown district of Powys formed themselves into a co-operative for the sale of their wool, but the venture failed because the wool buyers, fearing for their livelihood, boycotted the sales. Farmers in Merioneth went one step further and in 1947 established *Y Gymdeithas Wlân Cyf.* (The Wool Association Ltd) with the dual aim of not only marketing the wool of its members, but also processing as much of that wool as possible in their factory at

Dinas Mawddwy. Owing to a series of unfortunate events the enterprise did not really succeed.

One of the biggest problems that had faced sheep farmers over the years had been the violent fluctuations in the price of wool. Like most commodities wool had traditionally been sold at international auctions placing it at the mercy of market forces. Between 1872 and 1888, for example, the price of wool fell by around 75%, largely as the result of increasing supplies of foreign wool coming on to the home market. Welsh farmers were not immune from such pressures, for example fine short wool sold at Carmarthen fell in price from 1/4½d per pound in 1868 to 10½d per pound in 1888. During the First World War wool prices were controlled, but the immediate post war years saw a return to a period of instability followed by one of prolonged depression. On the international market tops of the finest Australian wool which had climbed to 171d in 1924 slumped to 24d by 1933. Welsh wool followed the same trend climbing to an all time high of 54d a pound in 1919 before plummeting to 7¾d a pound in 1922. This was the period during which many Welsh farmers withheld their wool for a number of years in the vain hope of a recovery in the market. A similar pattern was repeated in the market following the Second World War. Finest Australian tops climbed from 50d in 1945 to 353d in the summer of 1951, but fell to 151d by the autumn of the same year.

Largely in an attempt to protect farmers from the effects of such violent price fluctuations the Government introduced a system of guaranteed prices for a number of agricultural products, including wool, the price of which was set at 2/1 per pound in 1948, the first year of the scheme's operation. Two years later, in 1950, the British Wool Marketing Board was established. This Government sponsored body had the responsibility for marketing almost all the wool produced in the United Kingdom. Every farmer with more than five sheep is obliged by law to sell his wool to the Board at a pre-determined price. This price is negotiated between the Government and the farming unions and is based on a formula which takes account of the guaranteed price and the market performance of that type of wool during the previous year. At the beginning of each season the Board publishes its price schedule which lists the agreed prices for each of the three hundred grades of British wool for the coming year. The farmer then takes his wool to a pre-arranged point where it is collected by the appointed agents of the Board. It is then weighed and the farmer given a receipt for the total weight of his wool. The wool is subsequently taken to a central depot where it is graded, and the farmer is paid according to the proportion of his wool in each grade. The Board then deals with the sale of the wool to the manufacturers. Over the years of its operation the system has proved advantageous to both producers and consumers. Farmers have benefitted from having pre-determined guaranteed prices for their product, and manufacturers have benefitted from having a reliable source of uniformly graded wool.

Wool—The Fibre

Types of wool

Wool is not uniform in character, but variable in type and quality between, and even within breeds. The British Wool Marketing Board lists over 300 types of fleece wool obtained from the forty or so breeds of sheep found in the United Kingdom alone. A Kerry Hill fleece for example contains the following types of wool:

1. Shoulders & sides: the finest wool used for tweed making.
2. Lower part of back: good quality, but not so fine as that from shoulders and back.
3. Loin and back: coarser and often tender. Mainly used for blankets and flannel of better quality.
4. Upper part of legs: coarse, often containing vegetable matter. Used for coarser fabrics.
5. Upper portion of neck: inferior quality, irregular in staple length.
6. Central part of back: tender in staple, but fairly regular length. For flannels and blankets.
7. Belly: short, dirty and poor in quality and often tender.

8.	Root of tail:	poor quality, irregular, often Kempy.
9.	Lower part of legs:	irregular, dirty and greasy with much vegetable matter.
10.	Head, throat, chest:	stiff fibres, often coarse and Kempy.
11.	Shins:	thick, straight and irregular.

Because of this variation wool has to be sorted before it can be used to ensure that each type of wool is used for the purpose to which it is best suited. Wool is sorted on the basis of:

1. **Fineness:** Fineness is expressed by a quality number within a scale known as the Bradford Count. Each value denotes the theoretical number of hanks of yarn (each 560 yards long) which could be spun from a pound of the wool. The finer the wool the greater the length of yarn that can be spun and consequently the higher the number. Starting with the coarsest wool which has a quality count of 28's the scale increases at irregular intervals to a maximum of 100's. At one time the numbers referred directly to actual hanks, but the correlation has now been lost and only a theoretical relationship remains between the two.

Wool is divided into three broad categories of fineness:

Merino: The finest wool with a quality count in excess of 60's. It is used in the making of the finest quality yarns and fabrics.

Crossbred: Quality count between 36's and 60's. Used in making of the whole range of woollen products with the exception of Botany and the finest baby wools.

Carpet: Quality count below 44's. Mostly used in carpet making although proportion is made into coarse cloth.

All British wools fall into the last two categories, and 35% of the total clip is used in the carpet industry.

2. **Length of fibre:** Wool is divided into two categories on the basis of its fibre length. The short wool is carded to make the fibres lie across each other before being loosely spun into soft, fluffy *woollen* yarns. On the other hand long wool is combed to make its fibres lie parallel to each other so that it can be spun into firm, smooth, more hardwearing *worsted* yarns.

68

3. **Colour:** The whiter the wool the greater the range of colours it can be dyed, and consequently the higher its value.

4. **Crimp:** The natural coiling of the fibres which gives wool its bulk, warmth and strength. Crimp is generally proportional to the fineness of the wool, ranging from one or two crimps per centimetre in the coarsest mountain wool to twelve crimps per centimetre in the finest Merino.

5. **Softness:** Very much a subjective measure depending upon the feel of the wool when handled. Softness is essential in specialist wools such as baby wool and other knitting yarns.

6. **Soundness:** Poor diet and an irregular food supply often results in breaks in the growth of wool which results in weakness in the yarn. Such wool is unsuitable for purposes where strength of yarn is necessary and it is removed from the fleece.

7. **Felting properties:** Some wool has a far greater propensity for felting than others, and this is separated from specialist felt making purposes.

8. **Degree of lustre:** Lustre is the sheen that is visible on the fibre. Lustrous wool is strong, but it is often resistent to dyes which detracts from its overall value.

9. **Impurities:** Raw, unwashed wool contains a proportion of impurities which may account for as much as 50% of the weight of fleece in some cases. Impurities are classified as follows:

a. *Natural*
i. Secretions	- Grease
	- Suint
ii. Excretions	- Urine
	- Dung

b. *Acquired*
i. Vegetable	- Burrs
	- Seeds
	- Twigs
ii. Mineral	- Sand
	- Soil

c. *Applied*
	- Branding agents
	- Dipping agents
	- Salves and ointments

Most impurities are easily removed by washing and scouring, but those that are not detract from the value of the wool and have to be removed.

The Advantages of Wool as a Fabric

Wool possesses a number of unique and remarkable properties which makes it superior to most natural and man-made fibres. The most valuable of these properties are:

1. **Warmth:** The combination of two of its physical characteristics makes wool one of the warmest of all textiles.

a. Wool is hygroscopic, that is, it absorbs water vapour from the air, and in so doing generates its own heat. Experiments have shown that it has a remarkable capacity for heat production, e.g. a woollen jacket weighing one kilogram, when taken from a warm, dry room to a cold damp one generated as much heat on the human body. Despite this, wool is highly resistent to wetting, and can absorb up to a third of its own weight in water without feeling damp.

b. Wool also has a remarkable capacity for retaining heat, both that produced by the human body and that produced by itself. Its physical structure is such that it forms a large surface area which traps a great deal of air. As air is one of the most efficient insulators it prevents the escape of body heat through the cloth. A second insulating layer of air is also formed between a woollen garment and the body, because wool unlike many other fibres does not cling to the skin.

2. **Strength and Durability:** Wool possesses a high degree of resilience and strength again due to its peculiar physical structure. Each individual fibre is crimped, that is, it is coiled like a spring. It also acts in the same way as a spring in that after it is stretched it returns to its original length. It is this natural elasticity which allows woollen garments to retain their shape despite being stretched. Related to this is wool's durability, for despite the fact that it is practically the weakest of all fibres its elasticity gives it a strength equal to that of nylon. Crimp is such a valuable property in terms of strength, and warmth that it is inserted artificially into some man-made fibres.

3. **Felting:** Individual fibre structure also gives wool its felting properties. Each fibre is coated with angular plates or scales. When damp wool is agitated as happens during washing the fibres move towards their root ends. Having moved, the barbed tips of the angular scales catch on those of the other fibres and prevent them returning to their original size—causing the material to shrink. Shrinkage is a problem because carelessly handled material can be ruined, but it is also a property when carefully controlled that can be turned to advantage. It is this property which allows felt, a textile characterized by the densely matted condition of its fibres to be made. Controlled shrinkage is also used in tailoring to shape certain parts of a garment and slight felting of some materials, such as those used in the making of overcoats, has the effect of rendering them warmer.

Wool therefore has many virtues and many uses. It is almost perfect as a coat for the sheep, protecting it equally from the rays of the desert sun and the snow and rain of the Welsh mountains. The same natural properties of shedding water and insulating against the extremes of climate make it equally valuable as clothing for man. Other qualities such as durability, lustre, and facility to take dye makes it suitable for a host of other uses ranging from carpeting to industrial belting. Wool comes in so many forms that there is a variety for practically every purpose, making it one of the most useful fibres known to man.

Wool Characteristics of Welsh Sheep
(as issued by the British Wool Marketing Board)

Breed	Fineness (Bradford Count)	Average fleece weight (lb) (Kg)	Average length of staple (in) (cm)	Demi or Lustre	Main uses
Beulah Speckled	44-48	3-4 1½ 1-2	3-4 8-10	Flat	Tweed, Carpets
Black Welsh Mountain	48-54	3	3-4	Demi	Speciality, or black and brown yarns
Cheviot (No specific information available for Brecknock Hill Cheviot.)	48-56	4-5 2-2½	4 10	Demi	Tweeds, high class hosiery
Clun Forest	56-58	5-7	4	Demi	Hosiery & knitting yarns and felts.
Kerry Hill	53-56	5	4	Demi	Hosiery & knitting yarns and felts.
Llanwenog	56-58	5	3	Demi-Grey	Hosiery, handknitting tweeds
Llŷn	No Information Available				
Radnor	48-56	4-5 2-2½	2-6 5-15		Tweeds, flannels
South Wales Mountain	40-50	3 1¼-1½	3-4 8-10	Demi	Carpets
Torddu	No Information Available				
Welsh Half-bred	48-54	6-7 2¾-3	5-6 13-15	Demi	Hosiery, handknitting
Welsh Mountain	36-50	3 1¼-1½	2-4 5-10	Demi	Carpets, tweeds, flannels, blankets, rugs.

Select Bibliography

The following sources have been used extensively in the preparation of this booklet.

Alderson, L.:
The Observer Book of Farm Animals. London, 1976.

The Ark:
Journal of the Rare Breeds Survival Trust.

The British Wool Marketing Board:
Wool Grade Specifications 1972.

The British Wool Marketing Board:
British Sheep Breeds: their wool and its uses.

Gale, E.:
From Fibres to Fabrics. Mills & Boon/Allman & Son, London.

Haste, N. B. & Ponting, K. G. (eds):
Textile History and Economic History: Essays in Honour of Miss Jula de Lacy Mann.
Manchester University Press 1973.

Jenkins, J. G.:
The Welsh Woollen Industry. National Museum of Wales, Cardiff 1969.

Jenkins, J. G. (ed):
The Wool Textile Industry in Great Britain.
Routledge & Keegan Paul, London 1972.

Journal of the Royal Agricultural Society of England.

Journal of the Royal Welsh Agricultural Society.

National Sheep Association:
British Sheep, 1976.

Ponting, K. G.:
The Wool Trade. Columbine Press, Manchester 1961.

Ryder, M. L.:
Agricultural History Review volume XI (1 and 11) 1964, p. 1, 65 'The History of the Sheep Breeds in Britain'.

The Textile Institute:
Textile Terms and Definitions. Manchester 1975.

Thomas, J. F. H.:
Sheep. Faber & Faber, London 1945.

Thomson, H.:
Fibres and Fabrics Today. Heinemann, London 1974.

Trow-Smith, R:
A History of British Livestock Husbandry to 1700.
Routledge & Keegan Paul, London 1957.

Trow-Smith, R.:
A History of British Livestock Husbandry 1700-1900.
Routledge & Keegan Paul, London 1959.

Welsh Journal of Agriculture.

Zeuner, F. E.:
A History of Domesticated Animals.
Hutchinson, London 1963.